Helen Orme taught for many years before giving up teaching to write full-time. At the last count she had written over 70 books.

She writes both fiction and non-fiction, but at present is concentrating on fiction for older readers.

Helen also runs writing workshops for children and courses for teachers in both primary and secondary schools.

Making Tracks

by

Helen Orme

RanS⬤m

Making Tracks
by Helen Orme
Illustrated by Chris Askham

Published by Ransom Publishing Ltd.
Unit 7, Brocklands Farm, West Meon, Hampshire GU32 1JN, UK
www.ransom.co.uk

ISBN   978 184167 155 0
First published in 2013
Reprinted 2016
Copyright © 2013 Ransom Publishing Ltd.

Illustrations copyright © 2013 Chris Askham

A CIP catalogue

All rights reserve(etrieval
system, or transm
photocopying, re   ishers.

Accelerated Read   s of
Renaissance Lear   ed for
in the U.S. and o

The rights of Hel   › be
identified as the i   ce
with sections 77 a

Siti Musa

Wall · Photos · Friends

Hi! I'm Siti Musa.

Siti is a Swahili (African) name meaning 'Lady'.

I'm the oldest in my family. I have two brothers, Daudi and Hanif, and a kid sister Afia.

My dad is a deputy head at our school, which can be bad news sometimes!

My mum is a social worker.

Lu Clarke

Wall · Photos · Friends

I'm Lu Clarke and I'm an only child. My dad is a businessman – he has an IT office in the town centre. My mum, who is Chinese, works in a bank.

My mum's parents (Po-po and Gong-gong – our name for grandparents) live by the sea. They used to have a Chinese restaurant and my mum worked there when she was younger. My other grandparents live close to us.

My parents want the best for me – but they don't always ask me what *I* want.

Kelly Jonson

Wall · Photos · Friends

I'm Kelly Jonson.

My mum is a single parent. She works as a solicitor. I've got an older brother, Jamie. His girlfriend is Susie.

My parents split when I was very young, and Dad remarried. We don't have any contact with Dad and his new family.

I really want to be a writer – oh, and I fancy Gary! I've decided that I want to be a vegetarian.

Rachel Phillips

Wall · Photos · Friends

I'm Rachel Phillips.

My parents split about 4 years ago. Dad runs a small printing business, and Mum is office manager at our school.

I live with Mum and spend weekends with Dad. His new wife is Janine. They have two young children, a boy and a new baby girl. It's O.K. visiting them, but I'd rather be with Mum.

My older brother Wil is at sixth-form college.

Donna Mills

Wall · Photos · Friends

I'm Donna Mills.

My dad's a bus driver and my mum works in a shop.

I have two older sisters, Marie and Briony. Marie's friend Susie is Kelly's brother's girlfriend.

My brother, Michael, is the youngest.

I love animals and going swimming.

There isn't much spare cash in our family – which makes things hard sometimes.

Chapter
1

'I don't want to go. It will be cold and wet and horrible.'

Lu was moaning again. She didn't like rain.

'It will be fine when we get there,' said Siti.

'I'm looking forward to it,' said Donna. 'I think it will be fun.'

'Come on,' called Mr Jackson. 'Hurry up and get on the coach.'

They were off for a day at the local wetland centre. Siti, Donna and Kelly were looking forward to it, but Lu and Rachel weren't so keen.

'Come on,' said Siti. 'We can get the back seat.'

The trip took about an hour. By the time they arrived they were all fed up with Lu's moans.

'The coach will drop us off,' said Mr Jackson. 'Make sure you've got everything

you need. Don't forget your lunches and
rain gear.'

'You said it would stop raining!' Rachel told Siti.

'I'm not a weather girl. How would I know?'

'Yeah, but you did say … ' added Lu.

'I said it to stop you two from moaning,' said Siti. 'Grow up, the pair of you!'

That did it. Rachel and Lu were going to sulk for the rest of the day.

Chapter
2

They started off in the classroom.

'Boring,' whispered Rachel.

But it really wasn't boring and even Rachel and Lu forgot to moan.

By the time the session was over the sun had come out and things had started to dry up, but Lu and Rachel were still being grumpy.

They were split into small groups and taken to have a look round. Their warden was called Tina. She was young and really nice. She told them about the activities they would do.

On the way round Kelly saw some really strange animals.

'Look at those big cows!' She pointed them out to the others. 'I hope we don't get too close.'

'They aren't cows,' said Tina. 'They're water buffalo.'

'They look fierce,' said Kelly.

'Why are they here?' asked Siti.

'We rent out some of the land to local farmers,' explained Tina. 'Come and have a look at them. They are very friendly.'

She took the girls towards the fence.
When the buffaloes saw them they started
to move towards the fence too.

'Aw, they are cute really,' said Donna.

'Don't make any loud noises,' warned Tina. 'And if they turn their backs to you, move to the side.'

'Why?' asked Donna.

'If they're upset they spray dung at you.'

The girls moved away from the fence. Quickly!

Tina laughed.

'They are really good to eat,' she said. 'Lots of farmers are keeping them now.'

Kelly pulled a face. 'It's not nice to keep animals for food … ' she started.

'Oh, stop her someone,' said Siti. 'If she starts on that we'll never hear the last of it. Let's find somewhere for our sandwiches. I've got egg. Is that O.K. with you, Kelly?'

Chapter
3

After they had eaten, Tina told them about their task.

'We want to do a survey of animals that use the pond area.

First you have to visit the edge of the pond and note any tracks. You can draw them and we'll try to identify them later.'

'I don't want to go crawling around the pond,' moaned Lu.

'Let them get ahead then,' said Rachel. 'If they notice we can say we're following a set of tracks.'

They slowed down. Then Rachel noticed a side path. There was a bench not far along.

'Quick! Down here.'

'They'll notice we've gone.'

'Doesn't matter. We can hear them, and if they fuss we can say we went to have a look at something.'

They sat down on the bench. The sun was quite warm now.

'This is better than messing about in the mud,' said Lu.

Then they heard a noise. A rustling, coming from a reedy area nearby.

Lu grabbed Rachel.

'What is it? It might be rats.'

'It's a big rat then, making that sort of noise. It's just birds. There's loads of birds around.'

'Maybe it's those buffalo things. They've got loose!'

Chapter 4

'It can't be those. We'd be able to see them.'

'I don't like this,' said Lu. 'Let's go back to the others.'

Rachel wanted to see what it was.

'It can't be anything dangerous,' she said. 'Or they wouldn't let us visit.'

She went towards the noise. Suddenly she stopped and stared at the ground.

'Quick! Come and look at this.'

'What is it?' Lu didn't really want to go and see.

'Look!'

Lu looked. She shrugged her shoulders. There were large footprints in the mud.

'So?'

'It's a dinosaur!'

'Don't be silly,' snapped Lu. 'You're just trying to wind me up.'

'No. I mean it. I've seen pictures. It's a dinosaur!'

Chapter
5

Lu didn't really believe Rachel, but, all the same, she wasn't sure she wanted to go any further.

Just then there was a louder noise from the reeds and, suddenly, a small beaky head on a long neck poked up and started in their direction.

Lu screamed, turned and ran back, closely followed by Rachel.

It only took a couple of minutes to get back to the main path, where they met the others.

'Whatever is the matter?' asked Tina. 'Where have you been, anyway?'

'Looking for prints, like you said.' Rachel pointed down the path. 'And we've found a dinosaur!'

Tina looked annoyed. 'Don't be silly.'

'No, really! We found the prints, then we saw its head.'

Tina looked at Lu. She saw Lu was really scared.

'O.K. Stay here and I'll go and look.'

She'd only gone a little way. Then she started to back away.

'O.K.,' she said. 'Don't panic, but we need to keep calm and not scare it. It could really hurt us if we upset it.'

The girls looked at one another. Was it really a dinosaur?

Tina was getting out her phone. She saw their looks and laughed.

'Don't panic. I know its prints looked like a dinosaur's, and in a way I suppose it is a dinosaur relative. It's an ostrich!'

It wasn't long before the farmer arrived. Not only did he keep water buffalo, but he had an ostrich farm too.

He was really grateful that they had found his escaped bird.

'Tell you what,' he said. 'Come and visit my farms and I'll give you each a pack of ostrich sausages and some water buffalo burgers.'

Kelly was not pleased!

Siti's Sisters
The early years

– one year on:
the Sisters
are older

– another year on:
The Sisters have grown up (well, nearly …)